ICONS

History Makers

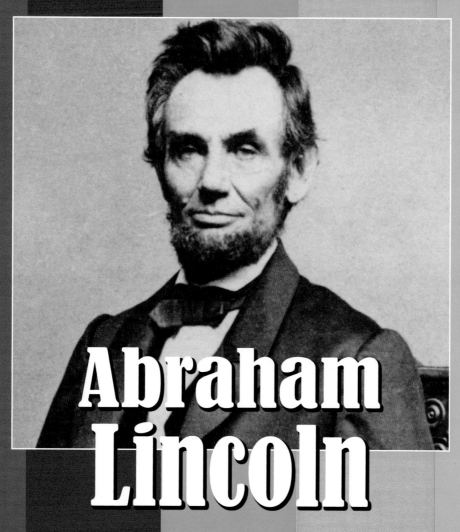

Abraham Lincoln

by Lauren Diemer and Megan Cuthbert

www.av2books.com

Go to **www.av2books.com**,
and enter this book's
unique code.

BOOK CODE

H 3 1 8 7 0 8

AV² by Weigl brings you media
enhanced books that support
active learning.

AV² provides enriched content that supplements and complements this book.
Weigl's AV² books strive to create inspired learning and engage young minds
in a total learning experience.

Your AV² Media Enhanced books come alive with...

 Audio
Listen to sections of
the book read aloud.

 Key Words
Study vocabulary, and
complete a matching
word activity.

 Video
Watch informative
video clips.

 Quizzes
Test your knowledge.

 Embedded Weblinks
Gain additional information
for research.

 Slide Show
View images and
captions, and prepare
a presentation.

 Try This!
Complete activities and
hands-on experiments.

... and much, much more!

Published by AV² by Weigl
350 5th Avenue, 59th Floor
New York, NY 10118

www.av2books.com   www.weigl.com

Library of Congress Cataloging-in-Publication Data

Diemer, Lauren.
 Abraham Lincoln / Lauren Diemer and Megan Cuthbert.
    pages cm. -- (Icons)
 Includes index.
 ISBN 978-1-62127-308-0 (hardcover : alkaline paper) -- ISBN 978-1-
62127-314-1 (softcover : alkaline paper)
 1. Lincoln, Abraham, 1809-1865--Juvenile literature. 2. Presidents--
United States--Biography--Juvenile literature. I. Cuthbert, Megan. II.
Title.
 E457.905.D53 2014
 973.7092--dc23
 [B]
                              2012041046

Printed in the United States of America in North Mankato, Minnesota
1 2 3 4 5 6 7 8 9 0   17 16 15 14 13

WEP040413
052013

Editor: Megan Cuthbert
Design: Tammy West

Photograph Credits
Weigl acknowledges Getty Images as the primary image supplier for
this title. Every reasonable effort has been made to trace ownership and
to obtain permission to reprint copyright material. The publishers would
be pleased to have any errors or omissions brought to their attention so
that they may be corrected in subsequent printings.

Contents

Who Was Abraham Lincoln?

Abraham Lincoln was one of the most influential presidents in American history. He was elected as the 16th president of the United States of America. At the time, the country was divided over **slavery**. Abraham led the country through the **Civil War**.

Abraham was, above all, a **patriot**. He supported the **Union** and he believed that the United States was founded on the principle of equality. Slavery went against this principle. As president, Abraham fought to keep slavery from growing throughout the Union. He also struggled to keep the country together.

OF THE PEOPLE
ED THE UNION
AHAM LINCOLN
FOREVER

*"Those who deny freedom to others
deserve it not for themselves."*

Growing Up

Abraham Lincoln was born in Kentucky on February 12, 1809. His parents, Thomas Lincoln and Nancy Hanks Lincoln, were from Virginia. Abraham had two siblings. His older sister was named Sarah. Abraham also had a brother, Thomas, who died as a baby.

The Lincolns had a small farm in Kentucky. In 1816, the family found out they did not legally own the land they lived on. The Lincolns were forced off their land. The family moved to Indiana, where they lived a very hard life. Abraham's family was very poor. They lived in a shack and had to hunt wild **game** for food. Abraham had to work hard to help his family. When he was just nine years old, Abraham's mother died. Her death was very difficult for the young boy and his family.

Thomas Lincoln re-married shortly after his wife's death. Abraham's stepmother, Sarah Bush Johnston, was a widower with three children of her own. Sarah became very close to Abraham and had a big influence on his education. She noticed how eager the young boy was to learn and encouraged him to read.

◀ Abraham spent several years at Knob Creek Farm in Kentucky. The country's first memorial to Abraham was set up here, and includes a recreation of his birthplace cabin.

Get to Know
Kentucky

N

ILLINOIS

INDIANA

KENTUCKY

TENNESSEE

STATE SYMBOLS

Kentucky is in the south-central United States. It is called the Bluegrass State because of the bluegrass that grows in the state's fertile soil.

The capital city is Frankfort. It is only the 14th biggest city by population in Kentucky.

TREE
Tulip Poplar

More than four million people live in Kentucky.

BIRD
Cardinal

Kentucky is famous for its horses. The Kentucky Derby is a horse race held on the first Saturday in May.

FLOWER
Goldenrod

Practice Makes Perfect

In 1830, Abraham's family moved to Illinois. At age 22, Abraham decided it was time to venture out on his own. He knew that he did not want to work on a farm for the rest of his life. Abraham believed that learning and education would lead him to a better life.

When he was 23, Abraham and a business partner bought a store in New Salem, Illinois. The business struggled, and Abraham had to sell his part in the company. Even though the store was not a success, Abraham learned from his experiences and moved forward. His time at the store had taught him how to deal with the public. Abraham became well-known and well-liked in the community.

◀ As a young man, Abraham worked on the farm clearing land and splitting logs to make rail fences. When he later ran for president, Abraham was often called the "Rail Candidate."

Abraham thought about becoming a blacksmith, but his friend, John Todd Stuart, persuaded him to become a lawyer instead. Abraham turned his attention to the law. He learned everything he needed to know by reading law books. In 1836, Abraham was admitted to the **bar**. He started practicing law with John at a law firm in Springfield, Illinois. Abraham had plenty of opportunity to improve his public speaking skills as he argued his cases before the courts.

QUICK FACTS

- Abraham was a talented wrestler as a young man. He was in almost 300 matches, and he lost only once.

- Abraham Lincoln was the tallest American president in history, standing at 6 foot 4 inches (193 cm).

- Abraham Lincoln lost several elections for other political positions before he was elected president.

◀ Abraham partnered with William F. Berry to open a general store in January 1833. The store has been recreated at Lincoln's New Salem State Historic Site in Illinois.

Key Events

Even before beginning his law career, Abraham showed an interest in politics. In 1834, he was elected to the Illinois state **legislature**. He served four terms while he continued to build his legal career. In 1846, Abraham entered national politics. He was elected to the United States House of Representatives, but he served only one term. Abraham spoke out against the **Mexican-American War**. This made him unpopular with the voters. He decided not to run again. Abraham returned to his law practice in Illinois.

In 1854, **Congress** passed the Kansas-Nebraska Act. The Act gave each state the power to decide whether or not to allow slavery. It angered many people who wanted slavery abolished. The Republican Party was formed by people who wanted to end slavery. Abraham joined in 1856.

Abraham's political passion was renewed. In 1858, he ran for the Illinois State Senate against Senator Stephen Douglas. The two candidates took part in seven debates. The focus was slavery. Lincoln lost the election, but the debates made him famous around the country. He was chosen as the Republican nominee for president.

◄ The first Lincoln-Douglas debate was held in Washington Square Park in Ottawa, Illinois, on August 21, 1858. A statue was unveiled in the park in 2002 to commemorate the event.

Thoughts from Abraham

Abraham believed in equality, unity, and freedom. He made many powerful speeches in his political career. Here are some of his quotes.

Abraham's thoughts on writing.
"Writing—the art of communicating thoughts of the mind, through the eye—is the great invention of the world."

Abraham explains the importance of unity.
"...a house divided cannot stand."

Abraham honored the soldiers who fought in the Civil War.
"...we here highly resolve that these dead shall not have died in vain—that this nation, under God, shall have a new birth of freedom—and that government of the people, by the people, for the people, shall not perish from the earth."

Abraham believed in the importance of preparation.
"Give me six hours to chop down a tree and I will spend the first four sharpening the axe."

Abraham explains his approach to life.
"I walk slowly, but I never walk backward."

Abraham talks about the difficulties that come with power.
"Nearly all men can stand adversity, but if you want to test a man's character, give him power."

What Is a President?

▲ **A portrait of Abraham Lincoln currently hangs in President Obama's office in the White House.**

The president of the United States has many roles. The president is the **head of state** and the head of government. He or she is in charge of the country and the government. The president is also the commander-in-chief of the armed forces. He or she executes laws and appoints officials. The president does not have the power to make decisions alone. In order to create or change a law, the president must work with the other politicians in Congress to make decisions for the American people. The president is also a **diplomat** and must meet with leaders from other countries and negotiate deals.

There are only three qualifications that a person must meet to become president. That person must be at least 35 years of age, must have been born in the United States, and must have lived in the country for 14 years or more. A person must be elected as president by the people of the United States. A president is elected for a four-year term. A person can serve two terms as president, but no longer.

THE WHITE HOUSE

Located in Washington, D.C., the White House is the official home and workplace of the president of the United States. When a president is elected, his family moves into the White House. Every president since John Adams, the second U.S. president, has lived here. The White House is home to the Oval Office, which is the official office of the president. The president holds many meetings and briefings here. International leaders visit the White House to meet with the president. Many state dinners and events are held there.

Presidents 101

George Washington (1732–1799)

George Washington was born in Virginia. He became a well-respected military leader and was chosen as commander-in-chief of the American troops during the American Revolutionary War. He helped lead the Americans to victory in 1781. A new country was formed, and George was elected to be the first president of the United States. He helped guide the new country's **policies** and played an important role in drafting the **Constitution**.

Franklin D. Roosevelt (1882–1945)

Franklin Roosevelt was born in New York. He became president in 1933, at the peak of the **Great Depression**. Many people were without work, and companies were going **bankrupt**. Franklin introduced laws to help get people back to work. He was also president during World War II and oversaw the country's wartime operations.

John Fitzgerald Kennedy (1917–1963)

John Fitzgerald Kennedy, known as JFK, was born in Massachussetts. When he was elected president in 1960, he became the youngest president and first ever Catholic president. During his time in office, he was a supporter of civil rights. He also helped the country avoid a nuclear war with the Soviet Union. On November 22, 1963, John F. Kennedy was **assassinated** while on an official visit to Dallas, Texas.

Barack Obama (1961–)

Barack Obama was born in Hawai'i. In November 2008, Barack was elected as the first African American president. He became president when the country was facing financial difficulties. Barack and his government provided loans to businesses to keep them running. Barack was elected for a second term as president in 2012.

Influences

One of Abraham Lincoln's greatest political influences was Henry Clay. Henry was an important political leader. He held several positions in government and even ran for president. Henry was a great speaker with a gift for compromise. These skills were useful in politics. Henry was good at negotiating deals and **treaties**. Henry was against slavery, but he also wanted to keep the Union together. Even though the two never met, Abraham respected Henry Clay. Abraham built his own political beliefs on Henry's **ideals** and would often quote Henry in his speeches.

◀ **Abraham Lincoln occupied the third floor law offices in the Tinsley Block in Springfield, Illinois. Before William Herndon, Abraham was law partners with Stephen T. Logan until 1844.**

While Abraham was pursuing his career in politics, he relied on his law partner, William "Billy" Herndon, to keep their law firm running smoothly. Billy was nine years younger and had a very different personality than Abraham. While Abraham was slow and thoughtful in his decisions, Billy was impulsive. Like Abraham, Billy did not believe in slavery. However, he was more extreme than Abraham in his political beliefs. Billy was quite critical of Abraham, but the two remained friends.

THE LINCOLN FAMILY

In 1842, Abraham married Mary Todd. She was the cousin of Abraham's first law partner, John Todd Stuart. The couple's first son, Robert Todd Lincoln, was born August 1, 1843. The Lincolns had three more sons. Edward was born in 1846, William "Willie" Wallace Lincoln was born in 1850, and Thomas "Tad" Lincoln was born in 1853.

Robert was the only Lincoln child to live past the age of 18. Edward died just before his fourth birthday, from a suspected case of **tuberculosis**. Willie died at the age of 11, during Abraham's second term as president. Tad died at the age of 18.

▶ Abraham nicknamed his youngest son "Tad" because when he was a baby, he wriggled like a tadpole.

Overcoming Obstacles

At the time Abraham was running for president, the northern and southern states were divided over slavery. The South made its money producing crops for food and goods. Slavery was an important source of labor for farms in the South. The North did not agree with the South's use of slaves. The North wanted to ban slavery. This was a dangerous time for the Union.

When Abraham Lincoln was elected president in 1860, the states in the south were worried. They knew he wanted to abolish slavery. After his election, seven states immediately left the Union. Abraham believed that this was illegal. He tried to convince the states to stay, but he was not able to do so. Fighting started between the North and South. On April 12, 1861, the Civil War officially began.

▲ Abraham Lincoln visited General George McClellan shortly after the general led the Union army to victory at Antietam in 1862.

▲ On November 19, 1863, Abraham Lincoln delivered the Gettysburg Address at the site of one of the bloodiest battles of the Civil War. Abraham used the speech to honor the sacrifices the soldiers made for the causes of equality and unity.

During the war, Abraham had a hard time keeping what was left of the country together. Not all of the northern states wanted slavery abolished. Abraham had to keep these states happy while still following his anti-slavery beliefs. In 1863, Abraham issued the **Emancipation** Proclamation. The order freed the slaves in the rebelling southern states. The northern states were still allowed to keep their slaves. This compromise was a small step toward abolishing slavery.

The Emancipation Proclamation inspired many people to fight for the end of slavery. It also allowed African Americans to join the army and fight for their freedom. Many of the freed slaves from the South joined the Union army. Even more soldiers were now fighting for the North.

Achievements and Successes

On April 9, 1865, the commander of the southern troops surrendered to the Union Army. The South stayed as part of the Union, and the country remained united. In the months leading up to the end of the war, an **amendment** to the Constitution was being debated in government. The 13th Amendment would abolish slavery. Abraham Lincoln was on his way to ending slavery throughout the country.

On April 14, 1865, just as the Civil War was ending, Abraham Lincoln was shot by John Wilkes Booth. He died the next day. Tens of thousands of people watched as his body was taken by train to be buried in Illinois. On December 6, 1865, the 13th Amendment was adopted by the government. Abraham Lincoln was not alive to witness the end of slavery, but he was directly responsible for changing the laws of the country.

◀ Abraham Lincoln's second inauguration was held on March 4, 1865, as the Civil War was coming to an end. In his Second Inaugural Address, Abraham spoke of his hope for both sides of the conflict to come together in peace.

In 1922, Abraham was honored with a monument in Washington, D.C. The Lincoln Memorial honors his achievements as president, as well as the personal traits he displayed that made him a well-respected leader. Millions of visitors trek to his monument every year. Abraham Lincoln continues to be an important figure for equality and unity.

HELPING OTHERS

Abraham Lincoln spent most of his political career promoting equality. He believed that the ideals of the United States were set out in the Declaration of Independence, which stated "that all men are created equal, that they are endowed…with certain unalienable rights, that among these are Life, Liberty and the pursuit of Happiness." Slavery went against these rights. Abraham used his political power to help ban slavery. He was also concerned with equality for women. He was one of the first prominent leaders to suggest that women be allowed to vote.

▲ The walls of the Lincoln Memorial are carved with parts of Abraham's famous Gettysburg Address and his Second Inaugural Address.

Write a Biography

A person's life story can be the subject of a book. This kind of book is called a biography. Biographies describe the lives of remarkable people, such as those who have achieved great success or have done important things to help others. These people may be alive today, or they may have lived many years ago. Reading a biography can help you learn more about a remarkable person.

At school, you might be asked to write a biography. First, decide who you want to write about. You can choose a president, such as Abraham Lincoln, or any other person. Then, find out if your library has any books about this person. Learn as much as you can about him or her. Write down the key events in this person's life. What was this person's childhood like? What has he or she accomplished? What are his or her goals? What makes this person special or unusual?

A concept web is a useful research tool. Read the questions in the following concept web. Answer the questions in your notebook. Your answers will help you write a biography.

Writing a Biography

Adulthood
- Where does this individual currently reside?
- Does he or she have a family?

- What did you learn from the books you read in your research?
- Would you suggest these books to others?
- Was anything missing from these books?

Childhood
- Where and when was this person born?
- Describe his or her parents, siblings, and friends.
- Did this person grow up in unusual circumstances?

Main Accomplishments
- What is this person's life's work?
- Has he or she received awards or recognition for accomplishments?
- How have this person's accomplishments served others?

Work and Preparation
- What was this person's education?
- What was his or her work experience?
- How does this person work; what is or was the process he or she uses or used?

Help and Obstacles
- Did this individual have a positive attitude?
- Did he or she receive help from others?
- Did this person have a mentor?
- Did this person face any hardships?
- If so, how were the hardships overcome?

Timeline

YEAR	ABRAHAM LINCOLN	WORLD EVENTS
1809	Abraham Lincoln is born.	James Madison is inaugurated as fourth president of the United States.
1834	Abraham is elected to the Illinois state legislature, the first of four consecutive election wins.	Slavery is abolished throughout the British **Empire**.
1842	Abraham marries Mary Todd.	Massachusetts passes the first U.S. child labor laws that limit working hours.
1860	Abraham is elected president of the United States.	The Pony Express, a fast mail delivery service, begins running between Missouri and California.
1861	The American Civil War begins.	Serfdom, a form of free labor similar to slavery, is abolished in Russia.
1864	Abraham is re-elected president.	Ulysses S. Grant is appointed lieutenant general and commander of the Union army.
1865	Abraham Lincoln is assassinated.	The American Civil War ends.

Key Words

amendment: a change to the Constitution

assassinated: when someone important is murdered

bankrupt: when a business has no money and cannot pay its bills

bar: the bar in a courtroom where only lawyers and judges can pass, symbolic of a person's ability to practice law

Civil War: a war in the United States between the North and South, from 1861 to 1865

Congress: the assembly of the U. S. government, made up of the Senate and House of Representatives

Constitution: the laws that govern the United States

diplomat: a person appointed by the government to negotiate with foreign countries

emancipation: the act of freeing something or someone

empire: many territories or countries ruled by one central power or government

game: animals hunted for food

Great Depression: a time during the 1930s when there was economic difficulty because of a stock market crash

head of state: a person who holds the highest ranked position in a country

ideals: values or beliefs

legislature: an elected group of people who have the power to make and change laws for the state or nation

Mexican-American War: a war between the United States and Mexico over land, 1846 to 1848

patriot: someone who loves his or her country

policies: beliefs or actions that will be pursued by a politician or government

slavery: being owned by another person; not being paid to work

treaties: agreements between countries

tuberculosis: a lung disease

Union: the group of states that wanted to keep the United States together during the Civil War

Index

Log on to www.av2books.com

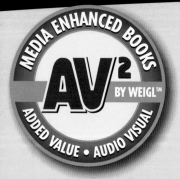

AV² by Weigl brings you media enhanced books that support active learning. Go to www.av2books.com, and enter the special code found on page 2 of this book. You will gain access to enriched and enhanced content that supplements and complements this book. Content includes video, audio, weblinks, quizzes, a slide show, and activities.

AV² Online Navigation

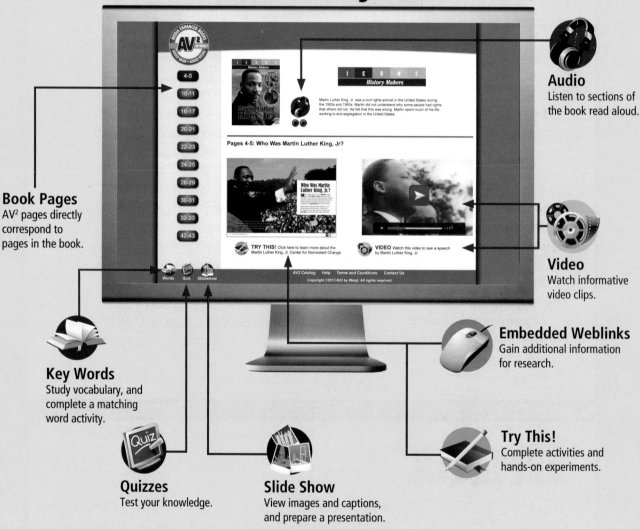

Audio
Listen to sections of the book read aloud.

Book Pages
AV² pages directly correspond to pages in the book.

Video
Watch informative video clips.

Key Words
Study vocabulary, and complete a matching word activity.

Embedded Weblinks
Gain additional information for research.

Try This!
Complete activities and hands-on experiments.

Quizzes
Test your knowledge.

Slide Show
View images and captions, and prepare a presentation.

AV² was built to bridge the gap between print and digital. We encourage you to tell us what you like and what you want to see in the future.

Sign up to be an AV² Ambassador at www.av2books.com/ambassador.

Due to the dynamic nature of the Internet, some of the URLs and activities provided as part of AV² by Weigl may have changed or ceased to exist. AV² by Weigl accepts no responsibility for any such changes. All media enhanced books are regularly monitored to update addresses and sites in a timely manner. Contact AV² by Weigl at 1-866-649-3445 or av2books@weigl.com with any questions, comments, or feedback.